S0-AQP-694

NEVER READ A
NEWSPAPER
AT YOUR DESK

The Fundamental Principles of Business

NEVER READ A
NEWSPAPER
AT YOUR DESK

The Fundamental Principles of Business

RICHARD F. STIEGELE

A Citadel Press Book
Published by Carol Publishing Group

Copyright © 1994 by Richard F. Stiegele

All rights reserved. No part of this book may be reproduced in any form, except by a newspaper or magazine reviewer who wishes to quote brief passages in connection with a review.

A Citadel Press Book
Published by Carol Publishing Group
Citadel Press is a registered trademark of Carol Communications, Inc.
Editorial Offices: 600 Madison Avenue, New York, N.Y. 10022
Sales and Distribution Offices: 120 Enterprise Avenue, Secaucus, N.J. 07094
In Canada: Canadian Manda Group, P.O. Box 920, Station U, Toronto,
    Ontario M8Z 5P9
Queries regarding rights and permissions should be addressed to
Carol Publishing Group, 600 Madison Avenue, New York, N.Y. 10022

Carol Publishing Group books are available at special discounts for bulk purchases, sales promotions, fund raising, or educational purposes. Special editions can be created to specifications. For details, contact Special Sales Department, Carol Publishing Group, 120 Enterprise Avenue, Secaucus, N.J. 07094

Manufactured in the United States of America

10 9 8 7 6 5 4 3 2 1

Library of Congress Cataloging-in-Publication Data

Stiegele, Richard F.
    Never read a newspaper at your desk : the fundamental principles of business / by Richard F. Stiegele.
        p.   cm.
    "A Citadel Press book."
    ISBN 0-8065-1560-0
    1. Business—Quotations, maxims, etc.   2. Management—Quotations, maxims, etc.   I. Title.
HF5341.S75   1994
650—dc20   94-16602

Acknowledgments

If I've learned anything, it's because I have stood on the shoulders of giants.

To my many bosses, mentors, and others who influenced my career in the North and South, whom I studied during my thirty-four years in the business world, and who provided inspiration for many of these thoughts: Dick Hall, Karl Ege, John McKenna, Jack McCauley, Dick Heinz, Bob Borgesen, Ed Kastner, Walter Myers, Sandy Halsey, Carl Klemme, Terry Flynn, Al Winiarski, Ed Gunnigle, Merle Volding, Joe Doran, Charlie Wingfield, Dick Good, Ellis Holt, Ronald Robinson, Cliff Harrison, Gene Southwood, Walter Hale, Rita Bennett, and my father, Frank Stiegele.

Particularly, to my long-suffering wife, Linda, and daughter, Cheri, who saw little of me during most of those years while I was overfocused observing these bosses and others and everyone and everything else around me in the business world.

I also thank InRoads USA's president and CEO, Charles

Story, and regional director, Mercedes Lytle, for asking me to make the presentation to the InRoads students in 1982 which was the beginning of this book. Thanks to Skeeter Davis, Leigh Wieland, Anne Cannon, Karen Jones, Sharon Bartlett, Darlene Rawls, and F. Tremaine Billings, M.D. And finally, I wish to thank Larry Stone for his expert encouragement. The following is a brief summary of what I learned.

Introduction

This simple little book is intended to be a practical, fast-read, pocket business mentor and primer for graduates entering the business world. It may also serve as a refresher for those more advanced in their business careers to ensure they are touching all the right bases in these lean, fast-paced, chaotic times. These are basic business survival principles which don't change. This is not the "Book of Revelations."

This list was first written in 1982 on three days' notice when I was asked to talk to some sixty college students about "corporate survival." There was nothing readily available in this format in bookstores, so I developed the list by jotting down the many things I remembered from various business situations under previous bosses and mentors—from first supervisors to CEOs in the North and the South who shared their experiences with me. It took two hours to present the original "Stiegele's 130 Laws for Corporate Survival or How to Avoid Downward Mobility" to the students since they had many questions. Subsequent presentations before many professional organizations averaged about twenty minutes.

The Laws caught the attention of the media, and a syndicated feature appeared in eighty-eight newspapers (Gannett) around the country in July 1982, entitled "It Takes Study and Analysis to Get to Know Your Boss." The piece was based on a four-hour interview and stressed that Stiegele "develops profiles of bosses." Although I had tried hard to say nothing that would identify the particular style of any one boss, the article occasioned many letters from my former bosses and considerable comments from present and past coworkers trying to determine who was who, particularly which boss needed to be buffered from those around him.

Surviving in business has been a favorite topic of mine, and the original list I compiled has been expanded over the years to the present 400-plus principles. Today there are library shelves full of books on various aspects of the topic, all of which take considerably more time to read. My premise is that if the principles are basic, concise, and clear, they need no further explanation.

The Fundamental Principles of Business

There are those in organizations who are known as survivors. In this chaotic era of mergers, acquisitions, divestitures, downsizings, restructurings, and bankruptcies, some survivors even survive their organizations. These are the things I think they learned and are doing right. Practice them, and your chances for survival will doubtless improve.

1. Don't spend a lot of time reading trendy business books. You may become educated beyond what is practical.

2. Don't try to be an expert on what you're not. Trying to write a symphony when you don't know music can take a lifetime.

3. Don't be a spin-master and overrationalize truth; practice "damage control." Admit you blundered, and how, so that the company can recover fast. Everyone makes mistakes, even CEOs. In today's dynamic, economic, social, and technological environment, everyone is learning.

4. Don't broadcast derogatory or confidential information that can hurt the corporation. Let somebody else do it.

5. Watch your expenses. Someone in Accounting is. The back of the plane arrives at the same time as the front.

6. Don't promise what your boss cannot deliver. In the end, if you fail, you make your boss the scapegoat.

7. Admit you don't understand something. Some may think they know it all, but no one is really expected to know everything. Ask for direction. It saves time, work, and frustration for everyone and may even eliminate your hearing the final direction.

8. Don't use "stressed-out" and "burned-out" as cop-outs. Learn to adjust to these chaotic times. It's never going to get any easier. Others have learned this and are waiting to take over your job.

9. Overcome daydreams about night things and secretaries.

10. Corporate efficiency decreases at the same rate corporate politics increases and businessmen turn into politicians.

11. Show respect for rank; your superiors earned it, one way or another.

12. Stay current on sexual harassment issues, particularly if you are overactive in this area.

13. Organizational charts are meant to show you the clearest route to the top.

14. There are always up days followed by down days in the business world. Just make sure yours aren't from uppers and downers.

15. There's either trouble or fun when workers gather in a group, never productivity.

16. Be friendly to coworkers, even if you're the Howard Hughes type. Encourage a "worker friendly" environment.

17. Don't be critical of the corporation unless you're the corporate auditor; your job may offer the only opportunity in town, and you may spend your life there. Besides, chances are, you sought employment there. Get out if it's bad.

18. Know how to listen and when to talk. Listeners learn more and see the big picture faster.

19. Don't brownnose to the point that radical surgery is needed to remove yours. Brownnosing will only achieve short-term goals. It will also be obvious to others.

20. Bad professional advice costs the same as good advice, but the greater the cost, the greater the chance the advice will be implemented.

21. The business world is an extension of the kindergarten sandbox—but with quicksand.

22. It's better to get a golden parachute than a golden handshake. But get it in writing.

23. Numbers may not lie, but they can sure do strange things if you want them to.

24. Don't leave time bombs for the boss when you go on vacation.

25. There is truth in wine. Don't outdrink others at office parties. If you're the boss, nurse your drink and leave early so the party can start, unless you've already had too much to drink and you *are* the party. And always drink diet soda at the "martini lunches." You never know who will be waiting for you when you get back to the office. If you're drinking like a fish, stay quiet as a clam.

26. Watch loose talk in the restroom. The boss may be reading a newspaper behind the closed door.

27. People work at the same speed as their boss, particularly if the boss isn't there; nothing motivates workers more than to see the boss sweat a little. If you're the boss, set the pace. Don't expect staff to work hard if your priorities are office furniture, company car, long lunches, and leaving early.

28. Tell lawyers what you want. It's their job to find a legal way to do it. And remember, the deal isn't closed until two weeks later, when all the legal documents are completed.

29. Read a good book on time management, make mental notes, and practice key principles. The basics of time management are learning to delegate and learning to say no.

30. Productivity is always higher on sunny days than on rainy days. Cheerful Muzak helps.

31. There are many who feel *The Prince* by Machiavelli is required reading for future managers. This is also why *Business Ethics* is a required business course.

32. Always talk to people the way they talk to you. They'll understand you better. And speak in layman's language no matter how technically educated you are.

33. An MBA is not an automatic pass to the top—unless you're working in the family business. There really isn't that much difference in human intelligence—how you apply yourself is what counts. Others may be naturally smarter, posses the wisdom of age, or have thirty-five years of on-the-job experience. There's always someone smarter and better qualified than you.

34. Take advantage of corporate stock purchase plans to feel a part of things, but keep up the payments.

35. Don't fight the consultants that senior management hired, lest *you* become part of the cost justification that pays for them.

36. Get to see the big picture quickly and learn everything you can about the corporation's personality—culture, objectives, key players, and house rules. Make sure you fit in and can make a key contribution, *or* get out.

37. Everyone makes mistakes. It's what you do *afterward* that counts.

38. Perform a self-analysis periodically to identify your strengths, weaknesses, and frustrations. If the analysis gets too heavy, seek professional help. List ways to overcome the weaknesses and frustrations and focus on them. This is a reality check and is called risk analysis.

39. Travel light. You'll get there faster.

40. The business world is full of different personalities. You have to work with them all. You don't have to like them all.

41. Don't watch the clock or spend time thinking about the great escape. Do one thing at a time if necessary, but consider it critical to the future of your job. Approach each task with a sense of urgency and give it your best shot.

42. "In God we trust"—and very few others. Get it in writing.

43. Expect change. That's all there is today. Be adaptable to it and try new things. Because the job has been done one way for years may mean it needs to be changed. However, if it isn't broken, don't fix it just for the sake of change.

44. Sell yourself. Nobody else will, unless you latch onto a corporate godfather. But promote your talents, not your ego.

45. "Pay your dues" by doing the occasional menial task. Even being the CEO isn't any bed of roses. (He has to get his own coffee when the secretary is out.) There's frustration, the mundane, the bad day at every level. That's why it's called *work*.

46. Behind every workaholic stands a spouse . . . and a mother.

47. Keep a copy of your job description, goals, and objectives handy to review periodically. If you feel underemployed, don't be limited by your job description. Work beyond it if you want to advance. There's always a new dimension you can add to your job. Learn to manage your own job.

48. There are no ready-made answers to today's complex problems.

49. Stay in your office and do the job you're paid to do lest you become known as a "professional floater."

50. Sharpen your communication skills. Senior management, with whom you have little contact, may judge you on your ability to organize and present your thoughts effectively.

51. Know where your career is going, but wait until the climate is right to talk career path with the boss. Timing is everything.

52. Plan ahead and then act; don't get in a reaction mode. But don't plan too far ahead; there's no such thing anymore as long-term. And remember, not everything happens according to plan. Be ready to adjust quickly to what is needed.

53. Work effectively. Always know your priorities and set realistic goals. Itemize projects on a legal pad, prioritize them, and focus on the A's. Keep the list in sight, and check it periodically with your boss to ensure you're on target.

54. Don't underevaluate your contribution. Don't overevaluate it either. Let others be the judge. Everyone's soon forgotten. Case in point: The thirteenth U.S. president.

55. Practice life management. Balance family life with business responsibilities. Keep pictures of your family in your office to help keep your priorities in order. Life is short, and success may not be what you expected when you finally achieve it.

56. Associate with successful people in your field. Use mentors (the higher the better), when starting your career. Then develop a list of respected colleagues you can use as a sounding board.

57. Always keep a pencil and pad nearby for thoughts requiring follow-through or to help remember good ideas.

58. "Brainstorm" a project with others. List all the issues and questions that come to mind, whether you're in the office or at home. Check the final draft against this list before signing off. And then have a trusted coworker review the final draft for feedback.

59. Offer suggestions for improvement. A small change on a much-used form can save the company thousands of dollars a year. Do your research thoroughly, however, and make sure your job isn't included in your savings projection.

60. Get involved in outside activities that help your corporation and community. Be realistic about the time and energy required so that your involvement won't diminish your job performance.

61. Know your sleeping requirements. Be alert and consistent in your job performance each day. Don't stay out until 3:00 A.M. the night before a big meeting and not be in top form. Others will notice when you are less effective.

62. Use your executive planner to pencil in important daily happenings, such as the implementation of a new procedure, installation of new equipment, a newly arrived or departed worker, your vacation and sick days, etc.

63. Never read a newspaper at your desk. It's a dead giveaway you've got nothing to do. Unexpected upper-management visitors might suggest specific pages of the newspaper for reading follow-up.

64. Maintain control of what you're doing, whether it's balancing cash as a teller or accounting for the assets and liabilities of a giant conglomerate as the CFO. And don't talk to the newspapers.

65. Be thorough. Cross-check details, especially if the information is going to senior management. An embarrassment for them might be a debacle for you. And follow through on important loose ends. That's the difference between an average job and a good job.

66. Never leave the office on Friday afternoon without looking at your appointment calendar to prepare for what's ahead next week. If you're on vacation, call in the day before you're due back to see what's on the agenda.

67. Don't be an armchair decision-maker and shoot from the hip. Get up and get the facts. Don't give personal opinions unless they are asked for. Business operates in a dynamic environment, and responses need to be timely and fact-based. Besides, fact-based decisions are hard to second-guess.

68. Don't give incomplete or wrong answers. If you don't know the right answer, find out and get back to the questioner with it.

69. Study your boss, her management style, what she finds important, her approach to problems and how much room for your own initiative she will grant you. Get to know what she expects, and anticipate her needs and priorities. Give her what she needs before she asks for it. For, not only does the boss influence the organization with her business style, but she also controls your salary and your future.

70. Don't play favorites or get involved in coworkers' lives, particularly if they report to you. Be fair and objective to everyone. Today's trainee may be tomorrow's CEO. Know where your coworkers are coming from, earn their respect, and make them feel important and part of what is happening.

71. Don't let others dictate your agenda for you. But don't work with hidden agendas. They'll become known to others sooner or later and you'll lose credibility with your coworkers.

72. Don't surprise a worker with bad news at review time; give feedback and address the problem before then.

73. Take care of your people and they will take care of you. Put others' considerations before your own and you'll find they will look out for you, too.

74. Lead by example. Be the first to try a new procedure or equipment. Your staff will know you understand their jobs and what you expect. Practice quietly first so you look efficient and adept.

75. Show appreciation for a job well done. Send a memo, letter, or flowers—not too many flowers, though. Clip and send items of recognition to those involved with the simple word "Congratulations!" and your signature. Everyone likes recognition, particularly from those above.

76. Morale and productivity go hand in hand. When one is low, so is the other. Be a strong manager and raise both. Demanding times demand strong managers, and the weak stand out. Learn to manage chaos.

77. Be tough but fair. Make the hard decisions when you have to. Your staff is watching and judging you. There's nothing worse than a boss who can't make a decision.

78. Don't get bogged down in petty infighting; the cast of characters changes too quickly, and you may have to live with the rest for your entire career.

79. Increasing the budget doesn't increase efficiency; probably inefficiency.

80. If you think it's a good idea, try it and give credit where due. You will get credit for getting it done. If it doesn't work, accept the criticism for it. And remember, praise is better than criticism.

81. Meetings are not a substitute for getting the work done. Never call a meeting if a telephone call or conference call can get the same results.

82. Defuse sensitive topics before a meeting to avoid unnecessary confrontation.

83. Keep meetings on time and on target. Prepare for them. (Few managers do.) Anticipate questions but don't over kill. Look organized, prepared, and confident. Use discussion agendas, exhibits, and hand-outs effectively.

84. Don't push for an employment contract if the company doesn't offer one—unless you're the new CEO. (Your employer may wonder why you need it.)

85. If you're the CEO and selling cost containment, you'll be more successful with a lean office image from which you can sell your program face-to-face rather than with memos.

86. Never upstage or criticize others in public, particularly your boss and those above you. Remember, everyone worries about looking smart to the boss—including *your* boss. Even CEOs have happy hours after the board of directors and stockholders meetings.

87. Don't overdelegate your responsibilities. You may delegate your job away in the process.

88. Listen for the boss's opinion and vote that way. Never vote him down, particularly in public. This increases job stress and destroys careers.

89. Bosses delight in changing memos—even if you have a Ph.D. in English. This is predictable and acceptable, and is called one-upmanship.

90. Go through proper channels. Bosses don't appreciate "end-runs," nor do their bosses appreciate being put on the spot.

91. Protect your bosses by all means. Keep them informed of things they should know to stay prepared for their bosses. Never let them be surprised with heavy, bad news first, particularly if it was your mishap that precipitated the crisis.

92. Give your boss your opinions. He or she expects them. But don't pepper your boss with questions from a just-completed project you know he cannot respond to yet. This is reverse role-playing—and imprudent.

93. Hitch your wagon to a rising star. Chances are, it's your boss and you can help each other.

94. Every corporation has at least one person who is difficult to get along with. Accept this as a challenge, and hope it isn't your boss.

95. Those best qualified don't always get the job. Family, school, and social affiliations sometimes get in the way. That's why good workers move on.

96. Being smart doesn't ensure success. Making the right decisions, getting the job done, and getting along with others probably will. Even top management isn't blessed with unlimited intelligence.

97. Don't oversell yourself in a résumé and job interview; truth prevails. Changing jobs doesn't automatically increase your experience and intelligence.

98. Don't buy personal gifts for subordinates. They could be considered part of a hidden agenda. Likewise, don't buy expensive gifts for the boss that will embarrass both of you.

99. Never send your résumé to a blind post office box. If you think you qualify for a job, it may be your own.

100. Some take top management utterances too seriously; others don't take them seriously at all, and that's why there's staff stress and executive burnout.

101. Enjoy the game you're in or change to one that's more fun. Your chances for survival will be better.

102. The higher you go, the more people you work for. Don't forget those little people when you've "arrived." They're holding you up there.

103. Surround yourself with people with winning attitudes and your chances of success will be high.

104. Be a leader instead of a manager. Managers supervise the status quo. Leaders make things happen through vision, energy, communicating, motivating, and taking chances.

105. People support what they help create. Encouraging participation and a sense of ownership will increase morale and productivity.

106. Don't sue a former employer if you want a reference.

107. Anticipate and do what those who control your destiny need. Don't waste time trying to satisfy everyone.

108. Never visit a former job. The day after you've departed, you're associated with all the company's previously undiscovered disasters. Your visit could well prove embarrassing for you and them.

109. All corporations have problems; things are never what they seem elsewhere. This is known as the "greener pasture illusion." Learn to put up with your troubles where you are and maximize your pension. Being tolerant can help pay the mortgage.

110. Don't overcontrol with too many procedures and reports, but don't undercontrol, either, and risk exposure. Both are expensive management styles and bring diminishing returns.

111. Don't spend your life on wordsmanship. Pass the memo along while it's still needed.

112. Get out of the office. Walk around and see what is really happening. Don't be limited to what you're told. This is management by observation. Besides, good news travels fast. It's the bad news you need to go after.

113. Strive to be the best in what you do. Become an industry spokesperson others call for advice.

114. Take a career aptitude test, talk with others, and then follow your gut feeling. Aptitude tests are even fun later in your career to see if things should have been different.

115. The numbers and types of careers are constantly changing; if you want job security, there'll always be a need for doctors, teachers, tax preparers, and morticians.

116. Smile a lot. It will make others more comfortable, particularly if you're the CFO. Your staff, instead of having to adjust to your moods, will be more relaxed and more productive. A manager with a good sense of humor can reduce stress and absenteeism and increase productivity.

117. Listen to "headhunters" even if you aren't interested. You may be surprised. You may also need them some day. Don't turn them off. Nobody likes rejection. However, be careful you weren't set up to test your loyalty.

118. Interviews are subjective and decided in the first two minutes . . . or less. Manage your immediate first impression. The rest of the interview is either spent firming up the hire decision or a polite way of saying "thanks for stopping by."

119. Always treat customers like they're your boss. They are! Talk to them constantly to be sure you are giving them what they want. Then produce it with quality, price it fairly, and get it to them fast. And remember, customer needs are changing as fast as the times. Don't be caught by changing consumer tastes.

120. Don't accept every outside request, don't see everyone who wants to see you, and don't return every telephone call—if you want to do a good job. Your time is limited; be selective with it. This is an important principle of time management.

121. Sabbaticals are for teachers, not burned-out business executives. Think twice before you ask for a sabbatical, even if you intend to take an extended management course or write a book.

122. Corporations have personalities. Yours becomes increasingly important as you climb the business pyramid. This is the often-talked about "chemistry" factor. Personality is the most critical key to success.

123. When someone asks you to keep something confidential, assume the request is genuine. You may otherwise ruin a friendship or a source of good information.

124. Trust everyone but trust no one. Today's friend may be tomorrow's enemy. And don't get too attached to people. They come and go quickly. There's little loyalty left.

125. At best, there is only a fifty-fifty chance a new hire will turn out the way you expected. Don't spend a lot of time on references. The responses will be predictable or they would not have been given as references. Even ex-bosses are relieved and gracious after they fire a worker.

126. Life is a series of changing multiple priorities. Flow with them. You need to be able to manage multiple priorities to succeed.

127. Don't make an assigned study your life's work, no matter how much you like the subject. Most often, studies are just to back up and formalize an initial management gut feeling for the right decision.

128. Don't schedule vacations in advance if you don't have to. Instead, take time when you feel you are becoming ineffective and need to refresh. But, in fairness to family and coworkers, be sure to take vacations.

129. Don't get hung up on titles. There are hundreds of thousands of others with the same title, particularly if you work for a financial institution. Titles are only important when you are signing legal documents.

130. While some people are clinical procrastinators, efficient people set their own deadlines and keep them. Approach everything you do with a positive can-do attitude. Your chances for success will be greater.

131. Your success is directly related to the time, energy, and thought you put into what you do.

132. Show patience with those less fortunate, and never be condescending. Make winners out of marginal workers. That's the real management challenge.

133. Don't go around saying or wishing it were Friday when it's only midweek. Stay focused.

134. Stay abreast of what's happening on your job so you remain the expert your company hired. Read. Be well read and well rounded in conversation. Attend evening classes if it's helpful.

135. Plan résumés carefully and watch for typos. Have your résumé proofread. And fill out job applications neatly. Busy résumés and untidy applications can result in instant elimination.

136. Always identify and prepare a successor so you can advance.

137. Talk to impress others, not to depress them.

138. If it's worth doing, it's worth doing right the first time, which is more productive and less expensive. *That's* the basic rule of quality. Teach quality. If you pay an incentive for productivity, discount for poor quality.

139. Always present several valid alternatives. What seems right to you may not always seem best to others.

140. Twenty percent of the people get eighty percent of the results. Pay for results and not just for showing up. That's fair to everyone.

141. Forget the telephone, voice mail, and fax machines. Go face to face whenever you can if the subject matter is important. Body language and graphology may be questionable sciences, but there's no substitute for talking directly with others and reading the signs.

142. Use simple, easy-to-understand color graphics wherever possible to make presentations more effective rather than handing out reams of paper and quoting long lists of meaningless numbers that will never be remembered. Keep it short. Just cover what you want remembered or done and make it interesting.

143. It's easier in the long run to fire difficult people than to live with them. Just be fair and be comfortable with your documentation. Don't live with "mis-hires."

144. Some confrontation is good to elicit diverse views and to ensure the best solutions. Have the courage of your convictions if you feel you have the right facts, but know when to back off and support what is decided.

145. Speak in simple terms and not in buzzwords. Others will appreciate it and be more impressed. Besides, who really knows the difference in "power" talk at "power" breakfasts and lunches.

146. New employees need a six-month learning period to find their way through the idiosyncrasies of a corporations' organization, systems, procedures, and people before they can really start to contribute. Be patient.

147. Be known as a creative problem solver and look for a fresh approach to what needs to be done.

148. Always put your name and date on every analysis you do—unless you're uncomfortable with it. If you are uncomfortable, redo the analysis.

149. Some things should be put in writing and some should not. This is a basic rule of corporate survival. Always let a heated memo or performance review season overnight before sending it or discussing it.

150. Always put a due date on action items or you'll seldom get results. But be reasonable.

151. List key interview questions beforehand, but don't purposely try to put candidates on the spot or at a disadvantage. You get to know people better if they are relaxed. Ask candidates where they want to be in five years to see if they plan ahead.

152. Hire a good, dependent, confidential secretary (administrative assistant) with good anticipation and follow-up skills, and use your secretary effectively. A secretary can make or break you. Treat her as an equal and a critical part of your own effectiveness. She is. And pay her well.

153. Always provide a way for others to save face. An out will work in your favor when needed. And it will be needed.

154. The bigger they are, the harder they fall, particularly CEOs, CAOs, CFOs, CIOs, etc. If top management fails to provide necessary leadership, it's easier to replace a CEO or the individual in question than all the workers, particularly in a larger company with hundreds of employees.

155. Prove yourself before you start making demands and telling management whether you will stay, particularly when the experienced incumbent could come back for your salary. And don't threaten to quit. Management may be waiting for your resignation.

156. Be up front and tell bidders who else is involved. You will probably get a more competitive bid.

157. Don't hide behind a memo, a letter, or a voice-mail message when delivering bad news. Going face to face is the fair thing to do. If you have to turn down a losing bid, give the reasons. The bidder spent time responding. If you have to fire someone, she has the right to know why.

158. Always tell people why you want to meet with them so they can prepare. It's fair and more productive and will get better results.

159. Don't ever criticize a coworker before a vacation and spoil a once-a-year diversion for him and his family.

160. Review the stacks of papers on your desk weekly and update and reprioritize your to-do list. You'll feel you have better control, and you'll be surprised at what you can eliminate.

161. Life is a giant user's group. Keep records of all of your business acquaintances in an address book with calling card holders. Make a note of spouses' and children's names so that you can ask about them. You'll use this source frequently as the basis for establishing your personal business network.

162. Never say it can't be done, or question why, and be identified as a negative person. You are paid to do what's asked of you. Work fast to figure how it can be done, and get it done before the next person does and reaps the benefit. Be known as a positive, can do person.

163. Don't try to change the world when you start a new job, particularly by telling everyone how good it was elsewhere. Wait until you really understand what is happening and why. But be a fast learner and an impact player.

164. Always request feedback and evaluate it objectively, whether it concerns service, product, project, or job performance.

165. Each business has its own dress code. See how the top players are dressed and dress accordingly. But remember, being a fashion trend-setter doesn't cut it either. Don't stand out by dressing like a country music star if you are Wall Street banker.

166. Show up on time every day unless you have a good reason. Don't have a spouse or friend call in for you. Your boss wants to hear from you.

167. No meeting is effective that lasts beyond one hour— unless it's a training session.

168. Train your secretary to screen, sort, and schedule your calls, meetings, mail, and, particularly, unscheduled interruptions. This is another principle of time management.

169. Focus on problem areas. Don't spend a lot of time on what is working well except to show appreciation to staff. There are only twenty-four hours in a day. Focusing on problem areas is management by exception.

170. Don't hide behind consultants to make your decisions. That's expensive, injures morale, and hinders creativity. If you have to use consultants, be open and prepare staff properly to avoid unnecessary conflict.

171. Always hire people smarter than you who can do things better than you—it shows how smart *you* are. Then give them the training, motivation, direction, and recognition to get the job done. And remember—you can't have just all-stars. That's expensive; someone needs to do the menial work, and that's why in sports there is a bench filled with role players.

172. It is smart to be an advocate of women, minorities, and those with disabilities in the workplace. They represent more than half the population and have the talent that provides greater ability to meet corporate objectives.

173. Know when to get involved with what is happening in your office and when not. But don't turn your back when you need to be involved because it's the easy way out.

174. Have short-term and long-term personal, financial, and business goals and review them periodically. Change them when you need to. It's a fast-changing world, and those goals all go hand in hand.

175. Don't oversupervise creative and professional staff with too much control, intervention, direction, and procedures, or you'll limit creativity, job satisfaction, and productivity. Focus on managing by results and not on controlling staff. But be available for consultation when needed. And take periodic checkpoints on critical, visible projects.

176. Don't be ambitious at the expense of coworkers or be a name-dropper that others feel uncomfortable with. Either one will work against your effectiveness.

177. Always know your next step in these uncertain times. Don't be surprised. Keep your résumé current and concise, and highlight accomplishments. Don't let your résumé become a lengthy autobiography. Be truthful: don't oversell yourself or be apologetic for a weakness. And network with influential people in your industry. That's contingency planning that will become crisis management if you are caught by surprise.

178. Learn the art of small talk, as hard as that may be. Talk fills uncomfortable silences and gives continuity to experience.

179. Watch the rumor mill. Know how to evaluate information and who to trust. Office grapevines can let you in on what's happening, but know your sources and what to discount. You may impress some with privileged information, but look at the risk. Use the rumor mill to your advantage in sending information or trial balloons.

180. Take one day at a time and try to do at least one positive thing each day. Give it your best shot. Your overall performance will take care of itself.

181. Everything is negotiable. Just know what you're negotiating, who you are negotiating with, and how bad you want what you are negotiating for. When the boss says it's non-negotiable, back off!

182. Get to know the organization's mission statement, strategic plans, and objectives and work toward them. They should be in the annual report.

183. Expect to pay your dues until you establish your own professional credibility. Work to continually enhance it and defend it if necessary. Credibility is built on getting along with others and getting the job done on time, within budget, and giving others credit where due.

184. Lock up confidential files at night so others don't copy and broadcast information that could compromise or jeopardize your relations with others or your career. Be careful what you put in the garbage. Rip up or use a shredder for sensitive papers.

185. Ask staff how to simplify their jobs or to solve a problem. They're closest to the work and know what needs to be done and what will work best. Simplify, simplify, simplify. Eliminate the unnecessary.

186. After giving a performance appraisal, always ask your coworker if there's anything you can do to help.

187. Teach your staff to think and offer solutions—not just to identify problems.

188. Instead of bulky, expensive policy and procedure manuals that basically exist to satisfy auditors and are never read, just publish the critical points that need to be observed and display them in visible places. In today's rapidly changing business environment, there is seldom time to read detailed policies and procedures that keep changing.

189. Don't carry extra baggage through life. Files build up quickly. Either discard a memo or report or pass it on with an action note or thank-you. Chances are slim that you'll refer to them again, and office storage space is expensive.

190. Don't accept gifts and lunches from vendors if you don't want to deal with them later. There are no free lunches, and it's harder to tell unsuccessful bidders that they lost if you've previously accepted their gifts.

191. Promote from within wherever possible—it's good for morale.

192. Never make promises, particularly long-term ones. Chances are you won't be able to keep them, or solve the problems caused by breaking them.

193. Solidify your base before you expand it, particularly if you are perceived to be a "turf builder."

194. Always have good reasons for what you do, particularly if you find it necessary to break the rules. Don't be afraid to take risks, but do your homework first.

195. Study everything about your CEO, i.e., personality, management style, and technique for dealing with others.

196. Accept the fact that not everything is going to be approved; you haven't much choice.

197. If your sights are really set high, think global.

198. Don't think of the weekdays as a good way to kill time between weekends. Be motivated by more than mortgage and car payments.

199. Ineffective managers form task forces to take the heat out of problems. But assembling a task force is often a nonproductive delaying tactic that indicates management's lack of problem-solving ability. If a problem is that bad, don't waste time with a task force. Talk it through and make the needed decisions on the spot.

200. Develop thick skin. Don't think everyone is talking about you and out to get you.

201. The best people always leave when the problem looks unsolvable. The rest have limited options, which makes it harder to solve the problem, which creates the need for the "new man" to bring in his own support staff. However, risk aside, problem times present the greatest opportunities.

202. More experience is gained from working in poorly managed organizations with constant crises than in those with no problems. Unless you welcome constant challenge and burnout, don't try to make your career in these organizations.

203. Get right to the point; time is money and success. Don't waste time on trivia and social etiquette. Say hello and ask the caller what he wants.

204. Return important telephone calls promptly, particularly any from your boss or top management.

205. Limit all memos, reports, and analyses to two pages or less (i.e., an "executive overview"). State the bottom-line results first. Highlight the key points. State the conclusions and the recommendations concisely. No decision is hard to make with all the facts clearly presented.

206. Reduce your communications to basic English and simple statistics, not lengthy and confusing narrative. It's more creative to write a poem than a novel. Don't use twenty words or several paragraphs if a sentence or one paragraph will do. Be conversational in your writing and eliminate abbreviations.

207. Don't waste idle time. Listen to audio books while commuting. Keep a cassette player and a notepad nearby to record follow-up thoughts.

208. *Big* isn't always best in business, but *quality* is. Focus on the basics and what you know and do best and expand in those areas.

209. Be ready to play hardball if needed, but always be fair, objective, and aboveboard. Then you will most always win the judgment calls in the clinches.

210. It's never too early to start saving for retirement. Your investment choices will be greater and the results more predictable.

211. There are A.M. people and P.M. people, and that's what allows you to meet production schedules all day. Know how to manage all types of people.

212. Experience has shown that the higher up an executive is, the more pleasant she is to deal with.

213. Today's mergers, acquisitions, divestitures, downsizing, and restructuring make corporate survival a high-risk game and career planning an unscientific process. Business careers are becoming a series of career redirections, interruptions, surprises, and varying projects. Expect to change careers and jobs more frequently in the years ahead. Only those who have the foresight to prepare, remain flexible, and are willing to adapt to change quickly will succeed. There are no lifetime jobs anymore.

214. Managers often have more authority than they think. Take the initiative and anticipate problems, needs, and trends, which are really opportunities to make things happen.

215. Your job begins anew each morning. Don't rest on yesterday's contribution if you want full retirement benefits.

216. The higher the position, the more intense the politics and risk. Everyone is out to topple "number one," and that's why salaries increase on the way to the top. Be adept at handling the psychological, social, and business forces coming at you. Don't ever be surprised.

217. The basics of office politics are becoming part of the system, i.e., getting along with others, satisfying the boss, and getting the job done. A certain amount of office politics is necessary, but keep it ethical.

218. To be successful, you need to be entrepreneurial. Encourage entrepreneurism in your organization.

219. In a merger or acquisition, study the acquiring company's culture and key management people. See where you can fit in—at least until you can negotiate a more desirable position elsewhere. Become an immediate team player and create a need for your services. Volunteer to participate on any change task forces and special projects. Be positive but realistic. But remember, the acquirers always say no immediate changes are planned to protect their investment during the transition.

220. Don't get bogged down in detail and trivia if you want to advance. Keep your eye on the "big picture" and make sure you are continuously learning.

221. The person brought in to turn an organization around almost never wins a popularity contest. If the reorganizing was insensitive, its leader is unlikely to find a following in the good times ahead, no matter how successful the results may have been.

222. When selling stock, leave a little profit for the buyer and you'll always be a winner.

223. Don't bring a friend to a job interview. Doing so is an immediate turnoff.

224. Know when to leave, particularly if you're the CEO. They'll remember you longer if you leave before a special committee needs to be formed to ask you to go. And don't become a dinosaur and come back second-guessing your successor.

225. Don't get caught between two top management members. Stay equal to all, *particularly* at that level.

226. Don't lend or borrow money from coworkers.

227. Always give the "suggested" amount to corporate-sponsored fund-raising campaigns. It won't get you promoted, but it won't hold you back either.

228. The best measure of success is salary, perks, and "other compensation." But job satisfaction is important, too.

229. Balance the need for short-term shareholder profits against long-term strategic plans and research. The future will be here before you know it, and you will be judged on today's success.

230. Many seminars and conferences make explicit what is already implicit and only provide extended paid vacations. Avoid being a journeyman conference-goer. The someone who has to do your work while you're gone may get the job done better, and you'll be expendable. Send for the conference cassette instead.

231. Choose to work for innovative and growing companies with top reputations. They offer more opportunities for career advancement. Bring new energy and creative ideas to the job with you.

232. Be a good mentor and share what you have learned, good and bad, with those working for you so they can help you work beyond your job and advance.

233. If you're the owner, stay involved until you go public.

234. Focus on the things you most enjoy and do best. They may not pay the best but you will be more successful. And keep doing your best. It will be noticed.

235. Seasoned consultants and outside examiners are those with battered, expensive luggage and are not timid in conversation with top management, thanks to the speed of modern air travel. Watch what you say.

236. Don't take personal problems out on coworkers or burden them with your problems. Always be professional. They don't really care anyway. Besides, their problems may be worse and you wouldn't want to hear them.

237. Never hold back a good worker from a better opportunity—no matter how important that person is to you. If she's offered a better opportunity, she has earned it. Share in her success. You may have been responsible for it.

238. Don't be aloof. Be approachable. If you're the CEO or another top official, have lunch in the employee cafeteria often and with as many different staff members as possible. Mixing with everyone is good for morale, and you'll find out what people are thinking and what's really happening.

239. Judge performance on qualitative rather than subjective criteria. Tie salary increases to bottom-line results and not personal situations. Doing so is fair and objective to all.

240. When firing someone, allow him to save face and confidence. He will need it to make the transition.

241. Discuss the job description step-by-step with each job applicant and have him prove he can do the job. However, assure candidates that they are not limited to the job description, which represents only the basics.

242. Don't manage by fear unless you want to manage robots. This style is no fun for them or you. Inspire and lead rather than forcing results.

243. Demand the best from your people and expect it. Periodically rank all your staff members by job performance. Then list their salaries next to their names and see if you're getting what you're paying for. Protect your good workers. They're in demand.

244. Have an open-door policy. Don't close your office door unless you have to. A closed door immediately leads to nonproductive speculation.

245. Answer your own telephone and make everyone more effective. Avoid "telephone tag." Just say "no thank you" right away if it's a call you don't want. The number of unwanted callers will decrease.

246. Don't hide behind lawyers. Remember, it's your signature that goes on the dotted line.

247. See beyond the numbers and cost-containment techniques to what is best for your customers and staff. They are what make the business—in that order. Cost-cutting has a point of diminishing returns.

248. Don't be afraid to request a budget variance when there's a sufficient business case. Such requests are highly acceptable, even expected.

249. If you want to control your time, go to someone else's office to meet. You'll be able to leave as soon as you're finished.

250. Prepare for meetings with your boss. List key discussion points in order of priority. Eliminate the unnecessary, and make sure your notes contain needed information only. But don't wait for a scheduled meeting when something is critical and can't wait.

251. Anticipate problems and deal with them head-on. It's harder to get the snakes back under the rock after they've gotten out.

252. Don't use the title "boss." Refer to yourself as a "coworker" and to your staff as "associates." Staff members will appreciate it and feel more a part of what is happening.

253. Limit the number of your direct reports to about half a dozen. And limit your time to only a few major projects.

254. It's always the same people who ask for something. Don't hesitate when the remaining few eventually ask for favors, particularly if you gave in to everyone else.

255. Determine your most productive time of the day and plan your higher-priority tasks during that time. Accept the unpleasant and get it out of the way quickly.

256. A certain amount of social conversation is necessary and helps keep everyone working together.

257. Never give excuses. Don't blame mistakes on computer "bugs" and typos. Be honest. In these lean, fast-paced times, no one can complete all the work or do a perfect job anymore. Accept this, but still give it your best shot and make sure you have your priorities right.

258. Write down your goals, i.e., where you want to go either personally or as a company, and list the steps to get there. Put names and dates next to each of the steps, and start implementing them. That's the essence of strategic planning.

259. Don't ever delegate what you don't understand and wouldn't do yourself. Others will know. Staff members appreciate that you can do their job, and they will do a better job for it.

260. Your credibility is on the line when you give a reference. Pass on it if you can't give a good one. Be fair and objective when you do and try not to put it in writing.

261. Don't wait for work or talk about it; go get it and get it done. Do whatever it takes to get it done within reason. That's a key to success. You're judged on results and not your oratorical skills.

262. You don't always have to have lunch to have a business meeting unless you are a salesperson. Meeting in the office is more productive, less expensive, and takes less time.

263. Memorize your family's social security numbers and birthdates early on. You'll use them often on applications and benefit forms.

264. Middle managers' jobs require that they support, sell, and implement management policies and decisions—no matter how unpleasant. Support top management if you want to succeed.

265. Always get back to job candidates as soon as possible. Don't make them call you. It's important and courteous, whether or not you plan to hire them.

266. Send a positive welcome letter to new hires highlighting their strong points and anticipating their success. Ask them to call if you can help in their transition.

267. Don't sell any asset in a soft market if you can afford to hold it until better times.

268. If you are in a top decision-making position, don't ever make a decision based solely on how it will effect you personally. Chances are that it will be a wrong decision. Sound decisions are based on sound business principles and not on egos, power struggles, or personal preferences.

269. The business world seemed unaware of stress until doctors and industrial psychologists identified and started reporting on it several years ago. Now everyone has stress, but you don't need to experience stress meltdown. Join a health club and go.

270. Business fads come and go, but the fundamentals of business never change. There are merely current buzzwords and new ways to explain old techniques, both helpful in perpetuating trendy new books. However, no business book ever said managing would be easy.

271. Identify the nonproductive workers. See if retraining or motivation is needed. If not, give sufficient warning and specific expectations with dates. In fairness to others who are productive and watching, weed out the individuals who show no improvement.

272. If you are the boss, you will reap dividends and respect by letting staff members choose their vacations before you do, including the days before and after holidays.

273. If you want to run the business, you need to know how the business runs. Make sure you make horizontal in addition to vertical career moves.

274. Don't leave long voice-mail messages. Call back later if it's that complex.

275. Don't be overly concerned about your letterhead and calling cards unless you're the CEO or a salesperson.

276. Determine early on your business objectives and whether you want to be in a staff or a line position.

277. Study successful organizations to see what they're doing right. Talk to their customers and staff and learn.

278. Don't allow nepotism in any way if you want to retain your good people.

279. Don't allow personal use of company property by anyone, or everyone else will ask for the same privileges.

280. Don't say or write anything you won't want quoted, particularly if you ask to keep it confidential.

281. Don't get into political or religious discussions unless you're talking to the mayor or your minister.

282. You need to ask the right questions to get the right answers.

283. Everyone has a gimmick. Get one and use it. The world's a giant users' group.

284. Do your homework when seeking employment. Organizational cultures can be vastly different. And seek a position, not a job. The former will last longer.

285. Identify and maximize the potential in your staff. Motivate staff members to work beyond their potential. Not only will they succeed but you may not have to work as hard.

286. Defend your people in what they're doing if they're right. They'll be comfortable with risk and extend themselves further for you.

287. No matter how bad the problem or the message, if you're management, psych yourself up and project a nondefeatist, positive attitude and turn the situation around.

288. Document important discussions in minutes or "For File" memos and publish them to the participants. In managerial science, this technique is referred to as "cover your flank," since some conveniently forget what they agreed to. List follow-up items showing who is responsible and when.

289. Chances are, you'll spend a lot of time thinking about your boss or at least talking about her with your mate; honor thy boss!

290. There's life after work. Start preparing early for retirement. Find a good hobby.

291. You'll spend more waking hours with coworkers than with your family. Make sure you spend sufficient time with your family also.

292. CEOs don't drive Volkswagen Beetles. Watch your image if you have high ambitions.

293. Don't have personal mail, magazines, and newspapers delivered to the office if you're trying to project a workaholic image.

294. The "harder you work the higher you will go" is a myth, but working smarter may increase your chances for success. No one can expect hard work to guarantee job security and career advancement in these times.

295. If you want to convince your boss that you are healthy, don't schedule doctor, dentist, psychiatrist, eye doctor, and chiropractor appointments on company time. But get an annual physical.

296. The physical office environment and productivity go hand in hand second only to salary. Provide well-lighted office space with updated workstations, equipment, color schemes, plants, art, music, and climate-controlled temperature. Décor makes a difference. But remember, staff and furnishings expand. Monitor both so you can control these costs.

297. Provide style and substance in everything you do, but balance both.

298. State-of-the-art isn't always best. Let someone else be the "beta-test" site, i.e., guinea pig.

299. Don't try to manage the building of a new house out of your office. It will be obvious to all. Hire a general contractor, or you may end up working out of your new home with no way to make the mortgage payments.

300. If you really want to know everything that's happening or going to happen, patronize the company shoe-shine vendor. But watch what you say on the telephone when getting a shine if you don't want to be grist for the rumor mill.

301. Delegate so you have more time for planning and your own top-priority items.

302. Today's business success stories may be tomorrow's hard luck stories. Look at General Motors, IBM, Sears Roebuck, etc.

303. Top management resignations that are "effective immediately" for "personal reasons" so that individuals may "pursue other interests" are usually followed by reports of significant negative earnings and the board of directors' strategic plans to reverse them.

304. Not all management philosophies and practices are good for every company, and that's why boards of directors change CEOs.

305. See an agenda before you decide whether to invest your time in lengthy meetings. When you return from a meeting to find that you are unsure of what was accomplished, you know you have attended an ineffective meeting.

306. When you're in a downsizing environment, the luxury of time for thinking and planning is over. You're now in the implementation phase.

307. People have more knowledge, talent, and creativity than required for most jobs. Encourage them to use their talents, pay for the results, and help them advance.

308. List all the facts, options, advantages and disadvantages of a decision on a sheet of paper. Test them on paper first, then keep thinking and talking through them with others, and eliminate what doesn't work until the decision is clear. Otherwise, start with a new sheet of paper.

309. You can always get more done in a crisis, which can be a good time to make changes—but planning and speed are critical. Try to bolster morale while making changes. If you are the new boss, you may need to improve morale before you can increase productivity.

310. Be sensitive to staff acquired in an acquisition. Don't be condescending, patronizing, or deceptive. (Having been on both sides of mergers and acquisitions, I know personally that such behavior is ultimately damaging and unwarranted.)

311. Before looking to reduce staff through a cost-cutting program, look instead at growing the business. If this isn't possible, then be sensitive to those who remain. Restructure work responsibilities and eliminate what doesn't really need to be done to avoid work overload, poor morale, and stress. Reassure remaining workers about their security to the point that's practical.

312. Corporate cultures tied to CEOs will significantly change when a CEO leaves and is replaced by an outsider.

313. Large-size doesn't equal strength if a business is entrenched in bureaucracy, which slows its ability to communicate with customers and adjust quickly to what they need. That's why smaller competitors, who are close to their customers, grow into big companies and big companies downsize and have cost containment programs.

314. In today's complex environment keep trying to simplify your organization's hierarchy, policies, systems, and procedures—to make it easier for customers to deal with you.

315. Become a tactician rather than a strategist if your company is ready to file for bankruptcy.

316. You can't produce and sell every product to every customer. Specialize. Pick a niche in what you know and do well.

317. Good morale can't be bought long-term with titles, raises, and perks—but it can sure get the ball rolling.

318. When the problems get heavy, take a walk to cool off instead of popping off.

319. We start learning the value of business success at home during our pre-grade-school years.

320. Don't send résumés on fancy stationery or with your picture. And don't leave zany messages on your home answering machine when you send out your résumé. You may not sound like the professional person prospective employers are looking for.

321. The higher you go, the closer you're watched, listened to, and quoted. Watch what you do and say.

322. Commit to company goals not just personal goals. Be a team player and project a company image.

323. Everyone starts out with the same amount of time each day. Successful people use it best.

324. Being late for social meetings may be fashionable. Being late for business meetings is inefficient and discourteous to the other participants.

325. Learn to empower staff members to make decisions on the spot, but set parameters and train workers to have good reasons for their decisions. And remember, you can delegate the authority but not the responsibility.

326. Open communication will reduce gossip and improve productivity. It's good for communication and checks and balances to encourage your staff members to express their opinions, even on performance reviews and exit interviews.

327. Schedule staff vacations by seniority, to be fair and ensure work continuity. But ensure a sufficient number of key staff members are available to get the job done.

328. Try different jobs when starting out in the business world to find out what you want to do long-term with your career. But stay for a reasonable period of time to learn and have good reasons for leaving. You will be asked to explain both for the rest of your working life in job interviews.

329. Don't be so preoccupied with planning the future that you forget the present even if you are the firm's strategic planner. The future is built on the present. Don't drown in the think tank.

330. Business decentralization may cost more, but the flip side is that it may increase creativity, productivity, and customer service level.

331. Business is sensitive. It goes where it is best treated. Repeat business is a sure sign of success.

332. If you're undecided, sleep on it, but don't use that as an excuse to put off the decision. Just be right at least fifty-one percent of the time.

333. Although employee suggestions may appear to be thinly veiled complaints, treat each one as a constructive idea for improving the company.

334. Let important memos and strategic plans season before finalizing them to ensure they include all relevant thinking on the issues.

335. Don't spend too much time looking for the cheapest alternative. It can be nonproductive and more expensive in the long run. Quality and delivery are also important.

336. When bidding out significant acquisitions, include a noncustomer. Doing so may ensure that you get the best deal and gain a new customer.

337. Think of negotiation as problem solving together and you will be more successful.

338. When you've made your decision to leave, move on. Don't linger. Your employer may have already identified you as disloyal, a security and competitive risk, and have started the search for your replacement.

339. Get the game tools and display them (the rawhide attaché case and sheepskin meeting folder for image, the executive planner to show you're organized, a pocket calculator [particularly if Latin was your major], and a large neosurrealist print behind your desk to show you're a deep thinker).

340. Start reading contracts from the back forward. Some lawyers expect you to lose interest, and that's why legal documents are thick. A critical point may be strategically placed on the last page. And always make sure there is an "escape clause" in your favor.

341. Some don't plan their careers, but just let them happen; others take opportunistic chances moved by fear, boredom, a need for change, or an attractive new position. Plan your career and check often to make sure you are on plan.

342. Corporate office executives make decisions between themselves first, take bets, prod, and wait to see how long it takes middle management to confirm them so they can put the blame where it belongs.

343. Corporate staff "has-beens" are dubbed "troubleshooters" and are immediately sent down to bail out affiliates, never to be heard from again. Affiliate "losers" are given honorific titles and "promoted" up to the corporation, immediately sent out to seminars and conferences and never heard from again until their plane lands minutes before their retirement party. All this is in the name of managerial progress, which looks very good in annual reports.

344. Senior executives often have the capacity and stamina to sort through the difficult and see things in their simplest terms.

345. If Monday to Friday seems like one day for you and you spend the weekend sleeping and getting ready for Monday again, you're a workaholic and need to rethink your priorities and consider the others around you before it's too late.

346. Some firms consider it fashionable to retain prestigious consulting firms; others are hooked on consultants to confirm their decisions or to be lightning rods for disagreeable political projects. Both are expensive management decisions. Use consultants discreetly.

347. All free, brief consultant engagements that promise to look for cost savings potential always uncover sufficient opportunity to justify longer engagements, and they cause middle managers to lament to top management that they didn't know things were so bad until these guys showed up.

348. Consultants, vendors, and others selling their services will always plead to be the last presenters since they know that the last in is usually the first chosen. Participants know what questions to ask the last presenter, which makes them look the most intelligent.

349. Where a fee is to be tied into results, build in sufficient incentive to motivate others to negotiate the best deal possible or to perform at their highest level so both parties share in the greatest return.

350. Read with a pair of scissors and cut out or copy important pieces of information worthy of focus, the interest of others, or for filing to reread in the future.

351. Bad news travels fast. Go public and admit a significant blunder while you can still control the media and what you want to say. Don't wait until it's too late.

352. Periodically evaluate your own management style and make sure you are current with what is happening and needed.

353. Many temporary jobs turn into full-time jobs even for managers and executives hired for special projects or expertise. Don't be afraid to take a temporary job in an area you like if you can afford to or if you have to.

354. Carry information in your head, not in your attaché case. But don't be afraid to take notes when it's important or if you have a poor memory.

355. Be fair in your management practices. Attack patterns, not isolated instances.

356. Many problems seem monumental until you have all the facts. Get the facts, and the solution may become obvious.

357. If you're the boss, you need to hear negative opinions. Ask for the flip side so you have all the input needed to help make the right decision.

358. Give simple, understandable instructions if you want fast and clear-cut results.

359. If you were an only child, make sure you know how to compromise.

360. Pick the right people at the start and managing will be easier. But correct "mis-hires" in the probationary (i.e., warranty) period or you may increase the problem.

361. Corporate leaders are measured on the bottom line, (i.e., profits, return on investment, stock price, and staff morale).

362. When interviewing job candidates, stress practical experience over academic achievements.

363. Don't hang on to outdated products. Be competitive and give the customers what they need now as long as it is profitable.

364. Whether you're the CEO or only a department manager, take your company or department apart periodically and put it back together again piece by piece at a planning session or just on paper. Reduce the extra layers of management, bureaucracy, outdated systems, procedures, and products. Demystify and simplify.

365. New CEOs need to do a quick, complete, and objective study, identify the problems and clean them up fast (no matter how difficult), while those problems are still associated with the prior management. Employers are looking for action, not hyperbole.

366. Departments in a division of a large organization may have been grouped together because of the talents of a particular executive, and therefore, are subject to change when that individual leaves. Be prepared for organizational changes after a top executive leaves.

367. You can't be all things to everyone. Standardize your products and delivery systems, which will streamline your operation, simplify training, and reduce expenses.

368. Look past your decisions and plan for the impact of change. Try to look beyond change if you are signing leases, contracts, or are planning major purchases, so that you don't wastefully invest needed capital that may not be needed after the change.

369. Be honest in describing the job to candidates. It will help get a better fit. You need the right personality and skills. Rehiring is expensive.

370. Watch jet lag. Lay out a day if you are going into heavy negotiations at the other end of a long trip, particularly across time zones.

371. Job security is no longer a given from an employer. You must maintain current and above-average knowledge of your job, good interpersonal skills, and the ability to adjust to change and the needs of the job market.

372. Because of corporate downsizing and restructuring, opportunities for advancement are shrinking. Set realistic goals and time frames.

373. Promotions may be made more to accommodate corporate cultures than on competence. There are times you will need to understand this.

374. Use all the "reinvent," "reengineer," "restructure" buzzwords to "reorganize" your own career, particularly if you have been at it a long time. But you need to know yourself before you can know what you want.

375. Caution staff members not to spread rumors much less become the focus of them—doing so places liability on the company, can jeopardize their jobs, and even involve them in legal action.

376. The choice of using in-house staff or an outside source for a job is governed by three factors: cost, control, and quality. If you do hire an outside source, you may have to work harder to manage the job from afar and you may not be able to retrofit it again internally.

377. Managing staff diversity in the workplace has become a critical measure of a good manager. Be open to accepting, training, and working with all types of people. Hire the best people for the job, focus on teamwork, and productivity will take care of itself. Try to understand and appreciate all aspects of your staff, not just their ability to work.

378. Boards of directors have well-defined responsibilities these days. If you're not willing to accept the challenge and make a contribution, resign your position or don't accept the appointment in the first place.

379. These are the days of information overkill. Memory and retention is limited even for a computer. Focus on only what is needed. File, pass along, or discard the unessential.

380. The sign of good quality is customer satisfaction and retention.

381. Vacation allows time to get away from the clutter and stress of job and life and to think about what is working and what is not working and to make good decisions about the future.

382. Competition is driving firms to learn as much as possible about their customers and employees. Strive to know your staff and customers through surveys, focus groups and mystery shoppers.

383. The hardest part of changing jobs is changing corporate cultures and social networks, which require a certain personality, self-confidence, flexibility, and the ability to deal with change.

384. Watch becoming so lean that it leads to staff burnout, loss of job satisfaction, low morale, the lack of time for workers to think and plan and conflicting priorities between departments and staff. Such disincentives may lead to losing your best staff members.

385. The whole world is a service bureau. Everyone is here to provide a service. How well you do determines how far you get.

386. Change means taking risk to make progress. Encourage and allow staff to take risks and make errors. The alternative is to remain status quo and be surpassed by your competitors.

387. Involve the internal and external auditors in significant planned systems, procedures and control changes to get participation up front and reduce the risk of criticism later.

388. If you are the CEO, make sure you have constant open communication with your Human Resources director to make sure you have the right people and morale is good; with the CFO to make sure the company's profitable; with the CAO to make sure everything is operating properly on a day-to-day basis, and with your strategic planner to make sure you're ready for tomorrow.

389. Make sure there is a strong business case for buying a corporate airplane based on current commercial air travel expense, loss of executive time, and fatigue—lest scrutinizing shareholders at the annual meeting see the airplane as no more than an executive perk.

390. If you are traveling far in a small corporate airplane, and particularly so in mixed company, restrict your intake of coffee, soft-drinks, and alcohol, so that you don't have to ask the pilot to make an unscheduled restroom stop enroute.

391. Every company needs a mission statement and vision for the future developed by management and staff. The statement should reflect your flexible way of thinking. Commit your company's vision statement and strategies to a simple one page message; distribute it to all employees and encourage them to reread it periodically.

392. Gut decisions are made on the basis of your total business education and experience, but make sure they are supported by fact.

393. If you are the data-processing manager or systems analyst, make sure you listen to the users' needs and give them what they need to get the job done and not what you think they need. If you institute the latter, the results could well incur considerable loss and service-level problems.

394. Don't be afraid to take a chance on an upstart small, lean company in the bidding process, provided the principals are solid. Chances are the principals will be directly involved in your project and they will be more responsive to you in an effort to build business and obtain a good reference.

395. Don't be a business specialist and limit your opportunities and flexibility unless the job demands it. Be a business Renaissance person and keep your options open.

396. Don't discount older workers. The young may have more energy and work harder but mature workers have more experience and usually work smarter.

397. Be humble with success. A measure of humility will work more in your favor than expecting a higher level of respect.

398. Set up a responsive customer relations department and
have the CEO sign letters when needed. Log inquiries
by type and analyze them for required problem-
resolution focus. Follow up every inquiry in a timely
way.

399. Set up a responsive employer relations department and
follow up on staff problems and needs. Look for trends
and provide feedback to the Human Resources Director
and CEO.

400. Work with staff members to make their jobs interesting
and to ensure they feel part of the "big picture" and
show appreciation for a job well done. These are two
basic principles for good productivity.

401. If you want to be successful, always do more than is expected. Deliver more than you promise and before promised.

402. Don't downsize for the sake of downsizing and short-term profits and jeopardize the long term, i.e., strategic planning, research and development for future products, etc.

403. Nothing happens unless you take risk, least of all anything new and innovative. The biggest risk is doing nothing in today's fast-changing times. Be a change agent.

404. Become a facilitator rather than a supervisor and help workteams make their own decisions and achieve their goals.

405. Start preparing for your next audit immediately after the examiners leave. You can't cram for an audit.

406. Don't sign time cards blindly. The employee may not have put in all the overtime or may be out working on another job or committing a crime.

407. Develop trust in staff members before signing your job away on their word.

408. Hire only the staff you need and make sure they work. Don't hire MBAs where entry-level workers are needed.

409. If you can't hire #1, go after #2. They come from the same corporate culture, management style, etc.

410. Try to clean out your files at least once a year—preferably before year-end.

411. Develop an innate sense of urgency about everything you do.

412. Things never seem as bad in the morning as in the middle of the night. Wait until the morning to solve the world's (business) problems.

413. Send detailed information out sufficiently before the meeting so you can focus on the important points and make the decision at the meeting.

414. A challenged, hardworking, and focused staff usually enjoys their work and makes fewer errors than a staff with few responsibilities. Phase in increased responsibility and productivity to change a poor work culture into one that breeds success.

415. Beware of associating the company's image and future sales with a celebrity whose sudden, impulsive, and potentially self-destructive behavior may be captured on worldwide television.

416. No matter how hard you try to do things right for top management, the more problems you will have—since everyone will be trying too hard to please.

417. Be optimistic but realistic.

418. Telephone interviews with the right list of questions can be very effective since you get more honest answers and save time that might have been spent on an unnecessary office interview.

419. The basic principle of accounting is to make sure that the numbers show the results in the best possible light.

420. The basic principle of communication is to make sure that your audience understands and remembers what you want it to understand and remember.

421. The basic principle of marketing is to make the buyers aware that the product is available and convince them it is the best and that they need it.

422. The basic principle of human resources is to retain happy, productive workers who work together as a team.

423. To sell, you need to believe in what you are selling.

424. Be respectful to the bosses and the CEO's secretaries. They have more influence than many acknowledge.

425. Be professional and brief in a letter of resignation. It will be an official record in your permanent file. Save any criticism for the verbal exit interview. And then be courteous. You may need the firm as a reference.

426. If your company is being acquired, remember, the acquiring company never moves its headquarters to the city of the acquired company.

427. Try to choose new hires who will bring new customers, energy, creativity, and productivity that will add to the bottom line.

428. Give staff members sufficient notice of performance appraisals so they can also be prepared. Focus on productivity and not personal problems. Be sure to end the meeting on a positive note.

429. Give staff members the power to resolve customer problems on the spot rather than having to tell the customer they will get back to her. Establish an automatic dollar limit in the customer's favor. Just don't publish or broadcast it.

430. Don't be afraid to ask honest and intelligent questions about the position during a job interview. It will be respected and show your interest.

431. If you want to be known as a visionary, "step back" periodically to gain a wider perspective on the workings of the company.

432. Don't be afraid to ask basic questions to complete your understanding. Others are probably embarrassed to ask them. It is the mark of intelligence to question—CEOs do it all the time.

433. Arrive each day before your staff members to show them what is expected. You will find it to be your most productive planning time.

434. The second business day back after New Year's Day is the most chaotic day of the year. On the first day back, everyone tries to catch up from the work postponed for New Year's parties, football games, and recovering from hangovers. On the second day back, they try to catch up for the whole month of December's screwups.

435. Watch what you say on voice-mail messages since they are not retrievable. You could be embarrassed or compromised if the message is accidentally delivered to the wrong telephone address or if it is redirected to someone else.

436. Focus on only a few important projects at a time if you want to get anything done and done right.

437. Do your homework for media interviews in advance. Be organized, concise, accurate. Be conversational, but to the point. Practice if you have the time. And, if you don't want to see it in print, don't say it.

438. The best test of a new product is to expose it to the real world. Take time to test-market it thoroughly.

439. If you don't understand the question, ask the speaker to repeat it.

440. Writing business memos and letters is as hard for some as writing suicide notes and obituaries. If this describes you, take a college-level business writing course or find a book or cassette that enables you to teach yourself the "how-to's."

441. Keep your long-standing business name unless you have a situation that will offset the lost name recognition, goodwill, signage, and stationery expense. If you are acquiring a company, consider leaving the company's name unchanged. Don't let corporate ego or a hungry public relations firm sway your decision.

442. Don't take pills and a thermometer to work. Stay home if you are that sick.

443. If you are suddenly fired or outplaced, don't sign anything in haste that you don't fully understand without first talking to your lawyer.

444. Voice-mail systems should be used for a company's internal messages and not for customer contact. Staff members who take customer calls should be instructed to answer their telephones and never direct customers to voice mail during business hours.

445. Good systems staff eventually work themselves out of their jobs by simplifying and automating everyone else's jobs.

446. Treat customers as you would want to be treated yourself. You will retain existing customers and gain new ones through word of mouth.

447. Small companies are close to their customers, and that's why they don't need marketing surveys and R&D departments to tell them what their customers want.

448. Life is a series of chances. Even when you do your homework, you need luck.

449. Team players protect their coworkers.

450. Teach your staff to satisfy customers first, then top management. If customers are happy, top management will be happy.

451. Barriers are perceived as obstacles. Be a barrier-breaker and make things happen.

452. Staff in large companies are either technicians, professionals, or managers. Staff in smaller companies tend to be generalists and multitalented businesspeople. Prepare for your career accordingly.

453. You don't have to have a degree in computer science to use a computer. Leave the building and programming of computer systems to the data processing technicians unless you manage their unit.

454. The best way to control the future is to plan it. And remember, good things usually take time.

455. Managing has become increasingly complicated because of the speed at which technology changes, global competition, and work force diversity. But remember, managing will always require controlling the market, production, and costs.

456. Don't invent work. There is enough to go around for everybody. However, the tendency is to give work to those who will finish it without complaining.

457. Boards of directors should first question management about their vision and strategies for the future of the company, then ask how and when they will implement the strategies, and finally, monitor management's progress toward the realization of the corresponding goals.

458. When preparing to review a proposed company-wide procedural change, develop and distribute a simple questionnaire regarding the current methods. Develop strategies and recommendations based on these responses for an effective procedural change. Plan for the impact the change will have on all involved.

459. Never voluntarily sit in front of the desk of your superior in the corporate hierarchy. Level the playing field by eliminating imposed barriers. Pull up a chair to sit beside the individual whenever possible.

460. Develop a mutually agreed upon list of reasonable, measurable goals with each of your staff. Put them in writing so that each of you have copies. Check progress periodically. Productivity should take care of itself.

461. Executive privileges, i.e. expensive club memberships, dues and subscriptions, are perks and have become passé in today's world of cost containment. Don't ask for perks—you'll be leaving yourself open for criticism.

462. To stay successfully employed in today's job market requires that one be involved in a continual, lifelong learning process. Anticipate job trends and stay prepared for them. Take business or specialized courses, if needed. Never stop learning.

463. Don't choose a corporate lawyer from a city bus advertisement if you expect a high rate of success.

464. Remember you can't say the same things as an executive and management representative that you could have said as a worker.

465. There are a dozen or more people in every organization who are the real workers and the "glue" who keep the organization together and moving, and they are not all top management and MBA's.

466. If you want to grow your company, focus on being the best where you are located first.

467. Keep a shaver (toothbrush, shoe shine cloth, small sewing kit and a backup set of glasses and tie) in your desk (for emergencies and) to look fresh for late afternoon and evening meetings, particularly if you are an early riser. Jack Kennedy was aware of this, Dick Nixon wasn't during the historical 1963 Presidential television debate.

Index

(The figures in the index refer to entries, not page numbers.)

About the Author

Richard F. Stiegele was born in New York, graduated from Fordham University (B.S. in Education/English), Programming & Systems Institute, and completed post-graduate business courses at New York and Pace universities. He has held various auditing, methods and systems, internal consulting, and management positions in several large New York financial institutions, including the Federal Reserve Bank of New York, Morgan Guaranty Trust Company, Marine Midland Bank, NatWest USA, and is currently senior vice president and director of administrative services at Third National Bank in Nashville, Tennessee, a SunTrust Bank, Inc., affiliate and one of the largest banks in the country, headquartered in the South. He is director of NashvilleRead and chairman of the InRoads Nashville Pre-College Program.

Stiegele has written many articles on bank operations, business change, and the use of internal and external consultants. He considers himself an observer and documentor of the business "game."